Pet Bakery

Business Startup

How to Start, Run & Grow a Trendy Pet Bakery Business

By

Rebecca Rothschild

Publishing House

Cover design

Mary Perez

First Edition

TABLE OF CONTENTS

INTRODUCTION: MY SUCCESS STORY CAN BE YOURS, TOO

Artisan. Homemade. Dog Treats?

Those are words that perhaps you don't very often see or hear together. It might seem an extravagance to feed your pet fresh treats like this.

You may feel as if the food you feed your pet every day from his bowl satisfies all his cravings.

But today, more than ever, dog owners of all stripes are turning to homemade dog treats, very often specifically handcrafted for a canine's enjoyment. If you don't have a pet, you may not understand where or why this trend has begun.

Homemade treats for pets have always been available, and recently they've become more popular than ever before. Not to mention, this is not just another "crazy trend" Americans have temporarily adopted.

Homemade dog treats are so popular in the United Kingdom that you can even watch contestants include them in a BBC television program called The Great British Bake Off. Unlike most baking contests in the US, this British hit features chefs creating a range of dog treats.

Inspired by that British television show and love, more pet owners are making homemade treats for their furry companions. Fueled by the rapid spread of information on the internet, there are what seems like an unending array of pet recipes. It's never been easier to treat Fido and King homemade artisan dog treats.

And for those dog owners who haven't yet jumped into baking for their pets but are more than willing to buy gourmet treats, some of the best options can be found at places often called pet bakeries. Whether the bakery is online or in a physical retail establishment across town, pet owners, especially those who own dogs, are willing to spend a reasonable amount of money so their pet can enjoy a delicious treat.

More pet owners are developing the tendency to treat their four-legged friends with the same attention and appreciation as their children, for they have chosen to not have any of their own or are waiting for the right circumstances to have or adopt some.

Therefore, the next short steps from doggie treat to the doggie bakery are natural.

There certainly seems to be no end to what pets like to eat and what their "people parents" love to treat them to. The range goes from snacks and cookies to buns, fishcakes, and polenta bakes.

But the lavish display of love doesn't end there. Some pet owners are baking birthday cakes for their dogs, baked, of course, with their pets' favorite ingredients. Another reason for the rise in homemade treats is a growing realization that commercially bought treats contain dubiously healthy—if not shockingly dangerous— ingredients.

For those owners who want to ensure their pets have nothing but food and treat with the healthiest ingredients, it's really not a long jump to creating homemade treats. After all, you can easily see this as a natural extension of food-buying if you're already dedicated to organic and natural ingredients in your own diet and that of your family.

Listen to the concerns raised by a first-time pet owner after learning about the ingredients found in dog treats. "When I investigated only a handful of these ingredients," he said, "I was shocked."

I personally discovered there was a ridiculously high amount of additives in commercially-bought products.

If the additives themselves weren't worrisome enough, animals, just like people, tend to develop allergies to additives as these substances build-up in their systems.

It oftentimes happens that dog food treats get less attention when it comes to their ingredients. If you make your own food, then you're in control of what your pet is eating.

That's basically what motivated me to make homemade treats. We had just adopted Lady, a beagle mix, and for the first several weeks doted on her. One day, my husband chuckled at all the time and energy I spent on her and asked why I wasn't going the extra few steps and making her treats myself.

That was all the inspiration and motivation I needed– an off-hand, sarcastic remark from my husband. I began to scour the internet and found enough recipes to get me started.

I began making the treats with nothing but "people" food, and somehow peanut butter also ended up in the recipe. Because the ingredients consisted of human food, I felt I could taste them along the way to ensure the nuggets would be at least somewhat tasty to Lady. After I finished a batch, I would sit down with a fresh cup of coffee, put a treat next to it, and then doled a treat out to Lady, who refused to leave my side while I was baking.

Another day, my husband came home from work early while I was still baking, and as he breezed through the kitchen, plucked a dog treat from the plate.

Taking a bite, he complimented me, "I think these are among the best peanut butter cookies you've ever made. You might want to put just a bit more sugar in them though."

I made so many treats when I first started; I knew I couldn't feed them all to Lady. That's when I began to give them to friends and family members who had dogs. They were a great hit. The recipients not only appreciated the thought, but they loved the freshness of the food and how the treats were actually good for their pets.

Soon, pet owners I knew anticipated holidays because I would always include treats in their family gifts. After all, if we've learned one thing in recent years, it is that pets are important family members.

Well, you can probably guess what the next step is. Yes, I launched my own pet bakery. It took much cajoling from my friends and family, who all promised they'd help me in a heartbeat.

I laughed at their faith in me. My first thought was starting a company and not selling a single dog cookie. Slowly, though, I thought maybe I should give it a try. I had always wanted to open my own business. I felt though it was something that was beyond my reach financially, and I knew I couldn't come up with the money for many of the projects I had in mind.

It was when my husband finally suggested I start a business that I took it seriously. I mulled it over. If I was going to do it, I had to be all in. There was no waffling once I made the decision; I had to jump in even on a part-time basis knowing intuitively that I would succeed.

Once I made my mind up and got down to business, I learned everything I could about operating a pet bakery. I learned the pros and cons of all sorts of foods; I learned a bit about how to start marketing it as well as my options about the various paths to take.

Whether it was my attitude or my recipes, or even if the stars were lined up perfectly the day I decided, my business became wildly successful in a relatively short amount of time, and I became outrageously happy being in control of my own future.

What I did was nothing out of the ordinary. You can do the very same things I did and find yourself one day running a successful pet bakery of your own; You'll find yourself standing in your kitchen, which is where I started, and feel wildly successful.

But more than that, you'll also realize that you are outrageously happy.

My success can be your success story, too.

HOW TO USE THIS GUIDEBOOK FOR MAXIMUM RESULTS

When you review this guidebook, you'll discover that it's divided loosely into three parts. The first part reviews the art of baking treats for your pets. If you've never tried your hand at this, there's no time like the present. Amazingly, it's nearly an effortless process. Can you read a recipe? Bake cookies? Bake a cake?

If you answered yes to any one of those, plan on having one happy pet, because you're an outstanding candidate for making homemade treats, the type that is sold at five or six times what it'll cost you to make.

Once you realize how much fun this is– and how good it makes you feel because your dog appreciates it– then it's time to consider giving these treats away for doggie birthdays, as well as including the pets of family and friends in the gift-giving holidays, especially Christmas.

And what dog, after wearing that not-so-flattering Halloween costume, wouldn't love to be awarded with a trick-or-treat reward?

PART TWO – BRIDGE TO BUSINESS

Once you've learned about the joy of baking your own pet treats (and believe me, it really is a joy), then I'll walk you through how to convert this love into your own successful business.

A pet bakery business is a perfect enterprise that can be started and expanded in your own home, which—

as I'm sure you're well aware— can reduce your start-up costs. This is wonderful because it gives you a chance to make money, reinvest it in your business, and eventually take it to the next level.

The next level could mean an online presence, consignments at pet shops, pet grooming businesses, and other pet-related places. Or you may decide to open a small retail store for your neighborhood four-footed friends.

PART THREE – THE NUTS AND BOLTS OF A BUSINESS

In part three, I help you navigate the ins and outs of the legal system. I've broken this section into three broad categories. The first explains the much-maligned document: a business plan.
The business plan, as I'll point out, is as much your guide to a successful startup as it is a much-needed document if you plan on borrowing money to finance it. It's historically seen as a difficult and tedious document to pull together. The good news, though,

is that it is not as difficult as you may think, as you break the business plan into various parts.

The second section in this portion helps you decide on the corporate structure from which to choose. Should you create a corporation? Should you take on a partner or perhaps remain the sole proprietorship?

If you don't know what I'm talking about at this point, don't worry. It's not a decision that needs to be made today. By the time you're ready to choose the business structure you deem best, you'll feel confident to make a decision, then talk to an expert in this area.

Finally, I'll spend some time talking about state and local regulations. Since these regulations— from health to taxes— vary widely from state to state and even from city to city, there's nothing that I can provide you that can be written in stone. But I will do my best to lead you to the many resources the internet has where you can do your research so you can launch your business on the right track.

Trust me, if I can build a pet bakery beyond my wildest dreams, then so can you. And regardless of whether you've made your first pet treat or not before you pick up this guide, you'll soon discover that with each advancing day, you're becoming more of an expert.

Before you know it, you'll look at that financial ledger and know that you're successful. And perhaps it will even be time to kick start your business to the next higher, grander scale.

So, what are we waiting for? In the next couple of chapters, I'll talk about the need and growing demand for fresh, organic, natural pet treats.

CHAPTER 1: FRESH TREATS FOR YOUR PETS. WHY BOTHER?

If you think that including pets in your family circle, especially dogs, is gaining popularity, you're closer to the truth than what you may believe. Today, more than 35 percent of households include a furry friend.

Well, we used to call them "furry friends," but within the last several decades, dogs are being elevated to family status. This is proven by the particular way Americans are not only selecting better qualities of dog food, and by the growing market for doggie treats.

Compound that data with the increasing concern of many dog owners of the potentially dangerous additives and other questionable ingredients in dog food and dog treats, and you will see why many individuals are turning to homemade treats – whether they're baking them at home or they're buying them from others.

Other dangerous ingredients that have been found in dog food include mold and banned antibiotics.

It would be unfair to condemn all commercially sold dog food because a few companies are trying to cut costs. But, then again, many dog owners refuse to take any chances, and rightly so. Your pets are completely trusting and depend on you to provide them with healthy food.
It's horrible to think that treat that you reward your dog with may actually be slowly making him sick– or worse.

I know that many of you will read this and believe that these individuals are sounding an unnecessary alarm. But consider just a few of the facts and data presented below, and you may change your mind.

Let's turn the clock back about a decade or so ago, to the year 2007. It was in this year that there was an increase in pet owner complaints regarding their pets who experienced kidney failure. The one thing all these pets had in common was that the treats they were giving their dogs contained ingredients that were imported from China.

Chew on this. Three months into that year, in March, veterinarians treated 141 percent more dogs than the year before.

Much to the credit of many stores, they recalled these products, and soon the testing began. The tests revealed that some of the ingredients were adulterated with melamine as well as other contaminants.

The additives found in these foods and treats, in effect, inflated the protein content in an artificial way, including wheat and corn gluten, rice protein, along with a number of other fillers.

To give you some idea about how widespread the problem was, this situation was found in more than 5,300 different foods. The tragedy is that many of these foods were sold in popular pet food stores. After all, was said and done, hundreds of dogs had unnecessarily died, and thousands more fell ill.

Flash forward several years. There was a small, but troubling epidemic surrounding people and dog food. No, these individuals didn't eat the dog food— they were merely handling it. What happened was 14 of them died across nine states simply through handling the food intended for their pets. It was eventually discovered that the food was contaminated by salmonella.

Officials were able to trace the problem to the same plant in which toxic mold had contaminated the food in 2007.

There was yet another incident in 2013, in which several major dog food manufacturers recalled dog treats when the company discovered that their products were tainted with a trace amount of antibiotics that had already been banned in the United States.

THE ONGOING PROBLEM

It would be of little consequence to you, today, if all these problems were in the past and I could tell you that there is no more danger in commercially-bought dog food and treats. But, I can't assure you of that. While issues like the ones I mentioned might not be getting as much press, they by no means disappeared.

Let me show you what I mean.

To this day, the U.S. Food and Drug Administration continues to recall treats that have been shown to be contaminated not only with salmonella, mold, and even shards of metal.

Last year, in fact, the agency fielded more than 5,000 reports of a variety of illnesses all with one common link: meat jerky pet treats. This included 1,000 deaths of dogs. Most of these complaints are related to, believe it or not, chicken in a variety of forms, including treats, tenders, and strips. Other complaints included in this number were due to foods such as duck jerky, sweet potato jerky, and related treats that have the meat of some kind wrapped around sweet potatoes or dry fruit.

More stores than ever before— from your corner grocery store to large retail pet store chains— are taking the clamor of their customers seriously in this matter. They have not only removed jerky treats, but any treat made of rawhide as well made in China.

The problem is so prolific that the FDA has issued this warning: "Pet owners should be aware that manufacturers do not need to list the country of origin for each ingredient used in their products."

In some ways, this may negate a packaging claim that promotes their product as being made in the USA. This very well may conveniently ignore the products that were not made here, but rather outsourced to this country.

ARTISAN, HANDMADE TREATS

Homemade treats made by cottage industries stand in stark contrast to those made by corporations. Buying treats by known small companies is one of the the only ways to ensure your pet's health is not declining. Of course, unless you decide it's time to take your pet's health under your control.

Making treats for your pets can also begin to clear up their allergies and many of the intolerances they may have developed through the years. Baking homemade treats are also given a boost in popularity by the ever-increasing growth of allergies and intolerances in pets of just about all types, but especially in dogs and cats.

This is easily accomplished by avoiding making treats that have ingredients that aren't normally part of a dog's diet as much as possible. What are some of the ingredients you should avoid, then?

Believe it or not, the most common dog allergy is beef. But the list keeps growing; your dog could also be allergic to any variety of foods including dairy products, wheat, chicken, lamb, pork, fish, and even eggs.

This makes it all the more vital that, as a responsible dog owner, you pay close attention not only to the ingredients in your dog's food and treats, but also to what and how many of his treats he actually eats.

One of the easiest ways to check for allergies is to become a detective of sorts when you introduce new foods to your pets. In fact, when you introduce a new food to your pet, start with only one new treat at a time. Once you've introduced this, maintain a normal eating schedule for about two months.

This gives your dog's body a chance to get used to the food. If the dog is eating the treat with no evidence of allergies or intolerance, then you know that your pet is not allergic to any of the ingredients. Then and only then should you introduce another treat with different ingredients for another couple of months to see how your dog's body reacts.

How can you tell if your dog has allergies?

If your pet is scratching excessively, it could very well be due to an allergy. Another symptom of an allergy could manifest as skin or ear infections that never seem to heal and of course, if your dog is experiencing gastrointestinal problems, then you may want to review his diet.

Some vets encourage owners to try to prevent the emergence of these allergies by feeding your pet a varied diet and to give him probiotics while he's still a puppy.

If you plan on including treats that are either made from or are small bits of human food, then you need to know that not all of the food we eat is good for your pet. You may be surprised, in fact, by the number of our foods that are detrimental to your dog.

The following chart is a list of foods that are detrimental to the health of your four-legged family member.

Food	In What Way is it Toxic?
Alcohol	Many people love to allow their dogs to drink several laps of beer. But that's not a habit you should get into. Alcohol of any kind impairs coordination and breathing, and in serious incidents may lead to coma and even death.
Apple Seed	These seeds release a cyanide compound when eaten. Granted, it would take many seeds to poison your pup, but it's best not to get into the habit, to begin with.
Apricot Pits	Another source of cyanide.
Avocados	These contain the substance persin, which is toxic to canines. Symptoms of toxicity include constipation diarrhea, pancreatitis, and vomiting.
Raw bread and pizza dough	Yeast dough that hasn't been baked can expand in your dog's stomach, causing bloating. Symptoms of this include drooling,

	retching, and a distended belly. Other symptoms include an increased heart rate. In rare circumstances, this can cause death.
Caffeine	If you allow your pup to drink any liquid with caffeine, you may be contributing to his hyperactivity. Not only that, it may trigger a fast heartbeat in him as well as increased blood pressure. In addition, he may react with seizures and tremors. In rare cases, dogs have died from consuming caffeine. Call your vet immediately should you discover he has eaten coffee grounds.
Cherry Pits	These pits contain the toxin cyanide.
Chocolate	Of course, with its caffeine content, this should never be fed to your dog. But there's an even bigger problem with this: the poison referred to methyl

	xanthine. It may take several hours for the symptoms of hyperactivity, vomiting, elevated pulse, fever, and tremors to reveal themselves.
Cooked Bones	Though technically not poisonous, you should avoid giving these to your pet because of the danger of the bones splintering. Choking can occur, or the bones may block digestion.
Corn on the Cob	Avoid this food since your pet can easily chew and swallow the cob. Like splintered bones, this can block digestion which reveals itself in vomiting and diarrhea.
Raw fish	Raw fish, especially salmon and trout, are toxic to your dog. That's because these two types of fish carry the bacteria neorickettsia helminthoeca, which when digested can be deadly. It takes approximately five to seven days to surface, and symptoms include

	vomiting, diarrhea, as well as discharge from his nose. Cooked fish is safe for your dog, however.
Grapes and raisins	While these may be healthy for humans, these are detrimental for your dog. They can cause liver and kidney damage, can in some circumstances lead to death. Even an amount as small as one cup can injure your dog.
Liver	When eaten in excess, it can be toxic to your dog because of its high levels of vitamin A. The consumption of liver, in large amounts can cause excessive bone growth, especially in the spine and joints. Other symptoms include weight loss and disinterest in eating.
Macadamia nut and butter	This nut can trigger fever, a rapid heartbeat, and tremors.
Onions and	These two foods both contain sulfoxides and disulfides which can

chives	cause anemia and potentially damage red blood cells. Known as hemolytic anemia, its symptoms include general weakness, no appetite, vomiting, diarrhea, shortness of breath, and dark urine.
Pits and seeds	Such pits and seeds can include peach and plum pits, and persimmon seed. As with so many other pits, they contain the poison cyanide.
Processed foods	What we don't know about the contents of processed foods is the number one reason to keep these from Fido and Lady. For example, many types of chips contain onion powder and without a doubt more salt than what is healthy for your pup.
Xylitol	This substance is most often found in chewing gum as well as breath mints and many sugar-free foods. This can trigger insulin

	overproduction in your dog as well as kidney failure and perhaps even death.

CHAPTER 2: NUTRIENT CONTENT AND SAFETY, WHAT ARE A CANINE'S NEEDS?

20 dangerous foods for our rough collies

Onion — Chocolate — Grapes — Raisins — Seeds

Macadamia Nuts — Animals Bones — Potatoes — Rhubarb leaves — Broccoli

Green Tomato — Coffee — Tea — Alcohol — Persimmons

Baking soda and salt — Mushrooms — Nutmeg — Sugar free products — Avocado

What is the common theme among these letters: A, C, D, E, K?

Wait. Wait. Don't tell me. They're not all vowels. No? So, what is it?

Each of these letters identifies a vitamin. A vitamin that is not only necessary for your health, but also the health of your friend Fido. Of course, if you chose to be in charge of all of your pet's meals, this knowledge would be indispensable to you in order to keep his fur shiny and his energy robust.

You may not have even thought about Fido's nutritional needs, let alone his "treats." After all, when we walk into a bakery for our sugary treats, we all seem to throw nutritional content out the window.

You may be tempted to do the same thing when making treats for your pet. But remember, there are many foods made for humans that can be harmful to your furry family member.

What guidelines should you follow when you're making your treats– both for your family pet and for your potential business?

When you're whipping up a meal for your family, for example, you know the nutritional needs of people so well that you really don't need to think about which foods are healthy. Not only that but you also probably know intuitively which foods are truly the healthiest to include in the dinner or to treat your children– or yourself– to.

But with dogs, let's face it, you probably couldn't create a similar nutritional pyramid-like structure illustrating their nutritional needs. That's to be expected. We'll talk about the best ingredients to use in your dog treats.

In this discussion on nutritional needs, we will first talk about meats and vegetables separately as two large umbrella categories. Following that, we'll talk a bit about the specific vitamins that can be included in the treats for your Fido.

THE FIRST RULE OF THUMB

If you can remember the first rule of what to place in dog's treats, then you'll never create a toxic or even a less than healthy tasty treat.

Meat and vegetables. That's right. Those two categories of foods should be the bulk of the ingredients of the treats you make.

To bear down on that rule, about one-third of the treat should contain protein like beef, chicken, or lamb. The rest of the treat– or his diet if you're making his meals as well– should be made from vegetables and then a few grains.

Many pet owners love making liver treats for their dogs. They're thrilled their dogs love such healthy treats. Keep in mind, though, that something as apparently healthy as liver should be served in moderation. Vets recommend that your pet should eat no more than one to two liver treats a week. If you give him any more than this, you risk your dog's health being stricken with vitamin A toxicity. Talk about getting too much of a good thing.

Is liver really that rich in Vitamin A that the potential exists for vitamin A toxicity?

Yes and no. What do I mean by this?

It's possible for your dog to get vitamin a buildup from eating homemade treats. But the liver you include in these might not be the only problem. Step back a moment and examine what else you're including in his treats. If you're making the treats properly they should have an abundance of foods that are rich in beta-carotene and vitamin A.

Before we condemn liver, let's review a list of vegetables that are safe for your pet, this time with an eye to the amount of vitamin A they possess. Then you'll be able to see for yourself the true odds of Fido or King developing vitamin A toxicity.

Food	Amount	Amount of Vitamin A
Eggs	1 large	270 IU
Sardines	1 cup, drained	161 IU
Liver	3 oz	15,297 IU

Apples	1 medium	98 IU
Carrots	**4 g**	**668 IU**
Celery	1 stalk	180 IU
Spinach	1 cup	2,813 IU
Green Beans	10 g	938 IU
Seaweed, Spirulina	**1 tbsp.**	**40 IU**
Seaweed, Kelp	2 tbsp.	12 IU
Raw Goat's Milk	1 cup	400+ IU (estimate)
Sweet Potatoes	1 cup	18,869 IU
Pumpkin	1 cup	9,875 IU

So how can you tell if your dog is suffering from a vitamin A toxicity?

You may want to add some oil or minerals as well as other ingredients. Of course, when creating the treats, it's always best to keep in mind the age of your canine, the level of activity involved, and any other health needs.

Dogs are carnivores, as you probably already know. That means they are meat eaters. And while it's not a pleasant thought from our point of view, dogs in the wild didn't hesitate to eat the organs as well as the meat. This gives you quite a bit of liberty in choosing the type.

If you notice you've fed him something that may be producing an allergic reaction, you should refrain for a while from giving him these treats until you're sure what ingredient is the culprit.

WHAT ABOUT THE VEGETABLES?

Not all vegetables are created equal– at least not in your dog's eyes . . er. . . mouth. What is the best vegetable you could include in his treats? Carrots. Yes, indeed. Carrots are jam-packed with nutrients and vitamins. They're especially high in the precursor to vitamin A, beta-carotene. This low-calorie food is also rich in fiber, a necessary inclusion in your pet's diet.

Here's another great vegetable to include in the treats: pumpkin. That might not have been the first choice. And yes, I realize that technically it's not a vegetable, but it's every bit as valuable in Fido's diet as any vegetable.

It's valuable to your pet's gastrointestinal tract, that's to say her digestion.

Your pet's health could use you including green beans in any type of food you make him. Unlike your children, he probably won't turn up his nose in disgust. The only caveat you need to pay strict attention to is to be sure that the beans aren't salted.

Include spinach. First and foremost, this dark green leafy vegetable is something your dog needs for all the reasons we do.

Beyond vegetables, what else could you make sure are in your pet's treats? Why fruits, of course. You'd be forgiven if the thought doesn't pop into your mind. Certainly, when I first started making treats for my pups, I didn't realize how important fruits were.

One of all the best is the apple. As long as you don't include any seeds, you'll have one grateful and healthy dog. Just as apples are a great source of fiber for humans, they serve the same purpose for your puppy as well. An added advantage of including apples in his diet is that they freshen his breath.

VITAMINS

We've already talked about the need for vitamin A and the inherent possibility that you may inadvertently "overdose" Fido.

The next logical vitamin research is B. Interestingly, unlike vitamin A, there are various nutrients grouped together under the grand umbrella of B vitamins. As you probably know, we, as humans, have what is often called a "family" of B vitamins that are essential to our good health.

Your four-footed friend needs the same pool of vitamins for the same reasons.

Let's start talking first about thiamine, or vitamin B1. Fido's body uses this vitamin primarily to help energize him and regulate carbohydrate metabolism. It also plays a vital role in the health of your pet's neural tissue.

Of all the B vitamins, probably the most important of them is B6. This nutrient is the one that's responsible for your pet's glucose production as well as red blood cells and even the general working of the nervous system. But that's not all, B6 is also needed for a healthy immune system response and the stimulation of genes.

Pantothenic acid, widely known as B5, also is a member of the family of B vitamins. Fido needs this particular nutrient to help him with the metabolization of energy.

Finally, the nutrient folic acid is part of the B family. While it's also known as vitamin B9, it's seldom called by that name. This vitamin plays a vital role in metabolizing both amino acids and nucleotide metabolism. It\ also is essential in mitochondrial protein synthesis.

VITAMIN C

Without a doubt, there is no stronger antioxidant than vitamin C. The role it plays for our bodies has been known and widely appreciated for decades, and it works in much the same fashion for Fido. This nutrient scavenges the potentially harmful free radicals in his body. The result of this is the reduction of inflammation, which in turns slows down the premature aging of the brain.

The body of your dog can make vitamin C on its own in their liver. But there may be certain cases where supplementing their own supply can boost their health.

VITAMIN D

Called the "sunshine vitamin," vitamin D helps to balance a variety of minerals, among them phosphorus and calcium. Your pet's healthy and strong bone growth depends on an abundance of vitamin D.

VITAMIN E

Here's another nutrient that's at the forefront of his defenses against oxidative damage. Vitamin E is a fat-soluble substance that is also essential for the proper functioning of cells as well as fat metabolism. This vitamin is also needed to avoid muscle degeneration as well as reproduction problems.

VITAMIN K

Many of us have never heard of vitamin K or potassium. For human beings, though, it's a valuable nutrient in the proper clotting of our blood. Vitamin is also a fat-soluble vitamin. Your four-footed family member needs this nutrient for the same reason. Interestingly, if your dog accidentally eats rat or mice poison, this could very well block the ability of vitamin K to do its job. This then could lead to hemorrhaging or even death if left untreated.

ONE MORE VITAMIN

It's one we didn't mention at the beginning of the chapter but is just as essential all the same. It's an instrumental part of the phospholipid cell membrane. While you probably have never heard of this, its basic functions are to support healthy brain activity and the working of Fido's liver.

CHAPTER 3: ORGANIC VS. NATURAL VS. COMMERCIAL TREATS

Why an ingredient that's natural may not be organic. Why fresh homemade treats are good for your pet– commercial treats may not.

Abracadabra.

Now you see a natural dog treat. Now you see an organic treat. And wait. One more waving of the natural magic wand you see– a commercial dog treat?

The third option is possible. But I'm betting it's harder to find if you limit your search to the large corporate dog food manufacturers.

It's easier to find natural and organic dog food treats from smaller firms and easier yet if you visit a pet food bakery. Yes, it may even resemble the one you're considering opening.

There's only one snag in this area; many individuals believe that natural food is the same as organic food. That's just not so. Before you buy another dog treat for Fido and Lady, let's look a bit more closely at the difference– however subtle– in these two words.

To make this conversation easier to understand, I'm going to use an apple as an example. You'd agree intuitively that the apple is a natural product. After all, it doesn't get much more natural than growing on a tree.

Can you call this apple organic?

Now, here is where the definitions get a bit blurry. The apple certainly could be organic if the orchard grove grower didn't use synthetic pesticides on it. Once you spray it with pesticides that aren't considered natural and are full of potentially damaging additives, it loses its designation as organic.

For it to remain organic, it must not be given any pesticides or only those that are made with natural organic products themselves.

This distinction is the same as when you talk about dog treats. Let's say you've just whipped up a batch of dog treats and you have the wrapping and label ready to package. Your package proudly proclaims, "natural and organic." Is it really?

You can understand how it can be natural– made from vegetables, meats, and other foods straight from nature. But if any of those ingredients were subjected to synthetic pesticides, unnatural additives, or additional antibiotics given to the animals, you don't have an organic product in your hands.

So while it can be advertised as natural, it certainly can't be considered organic. It's important to keep this in mind when you're buying treats, making them for Fido and Lady, or selling them.

No FDA Certification

Unlike food for people, dog food and treats don't fall under the jurisdiction of the FDA. This means up until recently; dog owners took their chances when selecting pet food as well as treats.

That doesn't mean the federal government is completely tone-deaf or complacent about the current problems and potential troubles that could occur without proper regulations and certification. To this point, the USDA is reviewing standards in this area.

Several organizations have appeared that provide guidelines for natural organic pet foods. Some of these associations allow manufacturers to have their processes certified to give dog owners peace of mind. Included in this certification is a mandated regular review.

Let's take a quick look at some of these organizations that are currently being the watchdog (no pun intended) to maintain high standards for your four-footed family member.

AAFC – ASSOCIATION OF AMERICAN FEED CONTROL OFFICIALS

This organization works with the states so these political entities can have available guidelines to develop their own policies to regulate dog treats and dog food. AAFO does research so you can be sure that their recommendations are as new and as relevant as possible to today's market.

Technically speaking, this association doesn't have the power to enforce any of its guidelines on the manufacturers; the fact that these commercial dog food makers even listen to this group makes it clear that they are at least attempting to make sure Lady gets a healthy diet.

OREGON TILTH CERTIFIED ORGANIC OTCO

The group analyzes dog food to ensure that the food contains what the manufacturer says it contains. In effect, to get this certification, a manufacturer must live up to the claim of organic ingredients from start to finish.

OTCO holds rigorous requirements from the standards it applies to standards of production. It also holds on-site inspections and enters into legally-binding contracts with the companies who follow these guidelines and meet these standards.

USDA

We've mentioned that the USDA has no regulatory powers over dog food manufacturers at this point in time. But its goal of conducting oversight power of "people" food can contribute indirectly to keeping your pet's food healthy. This association can be of great value to you in your position as a pet bakery owner

If a food intended for human consumption is labeled natural, it must meet the USDA'S guidelines. This organization requires that the label on the "people" food explains what it is as well as all ingredients involved. They also have guidelines for the use of the description "organic."

Keep your pet treats within the realm of people foods marked organic and natural, and you'll have a good idea that, by extension, your pet's treats will also be organic and natural.

THE DANGEROUS 6

The following discussion talks about six dangerous additives, processes, and ingredients that have no place in your dog's diet. If you're currently buying your dog treats from a large commercial manufacturer, this list may keep you up at night.

HIGH-LEVEL AND EXTRUSION FOOD PROCESSING

You may not realize it, but even if commercially-bought dog treats have all the proper and high-quality ingredients, it's all for nothing depending on how the treats are made. If the treats are made with high heat to sterilize the food, you're in danger of losing all the good potential of the food.

The production process will destroy much of its original nutritional value. This is why, even if you don't make natural dog food, natural treats are essential to Fido's health.

Antibiotics, Herbicides, Pesticides, oh my!

The adverse effects of this trio have been known for a while, as they're also a danger to humans and can lead to chronic disease. But more than that, these additives have the potential to accumulate in your Fido's body, leading to even more health problems.

ANIMAL BY-PRODUCTS

If you've been sitting on the fence until now, wait until you discover what animal by-products actually mean for the list of ingredients. Bear in mind these may very well could be included in your pet's dog food: Feathers, hair, leather, gristle, fecal waste . . . Enough said.

Meat and bone meal— which is made out of ground bone, gristle, and tendons— are the cheapest ingredients that pet food companies can use. Unfortunately, these are also the least nutritious of all the by-product meals.

If that isn't enough, in addition to not particularly boosting your dog's nutritional status, a stunning quarter of the protein in these foods can't even be digested by Fido.

These animal by-products have also been shown to trigger canine tumors.

ARTIFICIAL COLORS

Commercial dog food contains artificial colors to make the food more attractive.

But more attractive to whom?

Let's think about this for a minute. While dogs are not actually colorblind, they do see a spectrum of colors that is limited compared to the one humans have. In the grand scheme of things, it can be safely assumed that a Great Dane would not mind if his or her food is purple or brown, so long as the taste and smell are worthwhile. Therefore, artificial coloring is more of a hassle than an actually beneficial ingredient.

If you haven't noticed, natural organic pet treats may at times look quite boring compared to their colorful commercial counterparts. That's because the emphasis is on nutrition and not enhancing its attractiveness to those who are buying the food.

Adding food coloring to pet snacks and food wouldn't be so bad if the coloring itself wasn't considered a threat to your Fido's health. The full results of the adverse effects have not been fully investigated yet, but what has been done seems to link artificial color with an increased sensitivity to viruses, and is suspected to be associated with cancer.

CHEMICAL PRESERVATIVES

Chemical preservatives are necessary if the food is going to sit on grocery store shelves and in pet stores. So, if you buy commercial food, you can be sure it contains at least some chemical preservatives. Depending on the preservative, here are some of the problems that could occur if Fido ingests too many of them.

Adverse effects of chemical preservatives:

Various allergic reactions	Behavioral problems	Chronic diarrhea	Dry skin that causes excessive scratching

Dehydration	Diabetes	Excessive thirst	Hair loss
Loss of good intestinal bacteria	Liver damage	Metabolic stress	Obesity
Reduction in the absorption of nutrients	Cholesterol level increase	Dental problems	

FILLER INGREDIENTS

These filler ingredients sometimes referred to as filler foods, aren't necessarily "bad" for Fido and Lady when they stand alone. It's how these foods are used in the food and treats that make them a danger to your furry friend's well-being.

The majority of these types of food are carbohydrates. In and of themselves, carbohydrates aren't bad, and they are certainly not dangerous.

So, why are they considered dangerous in dog food? That's because fillers for dog food are chosen from the wrong kinds of carbohydrates, including sugar and corn syrup. Even from only choosing these two you can see why many dogs gain weight and even become obese.

Filler, by the way, couldn't be a more apt term for these ingredients; they fill your dog up with unhealthy foods instead of on nutrient-rich foods.

This stands in stark contrast to natural organic dog treats, which use nothing but nutritionally sound foods. When your dog has finished eating, you're assured he's getting his nutrients for the day.

If you're beginning to try your hand at making your own treats for Fido and Lady, you should feel vindicated from those who try to give you a hard time about what you're doing.

Below is a chart which gives you a quick overview of what we've been talking about. It's a handy guideline to use should you begin to doubt if your homemade treats or the commercial ones you've been buying up are natural and organic. I've broken this down in three different areas: natural, organic, and commercial.

The first column indicates some of the items it may have been subjected to and still be labeled natural, organic, or commercial.

Of course, this chart is far from the final arbitrator of any label. But it does clarify some of the topics we've covered in this chapter.

Variable	Commercial Dog Food	Natural Dog Food	Organic Dog Food
High heat and extrusion process	Yes	No Guarantee	No Guarantee
Antibiotics	Yes	No Guarantee	No
Herbicides	Yes	No Guarantee	No
Pesticides	Yes	No Guarantee	No
Human-grade meats	No	No Guarantee	Yes

Animal By-products, i.e., blood, waste, "meal."	Yes	No	No
Artificial colors	Yes	No	No
Chemical preservatives	Yes	No	No
Filler foods	Yes	No	No
Genetically Modified	Yes	No	No
Grain Quality	Low	High	High
Meat quality	Low	High	High
Vitamin, mineral content	Low	High	High
Cost	Less expensive	Approximately half the cost of organic dog treats	Approximately twice the cost if commercially bought treats
Availability	Abundant	Possibly limited	Possibly limited
Alternatives	Natural, organic	organic	"People"

	or "people" food	"people" food	good is better overall

CHAPTER 4: EQUIPMENT AND SUPPLIES YOU'LL NEED

In this chapter, there will be a list of equipment that's most important and most used in baking a variety of pet treats.

Making pet treats from your home– whether to use and gift or to sell– means you're already reducing costs, as opposed to opening a retail store. Unlike most at-home businesses, you'll need very specialized equipment to make your initial treats. That doesn't mean, though, that you may not want to invest in a few long-lasting mixers as your business evolves.

Even before you begin selling the treats, you may want to at least browse– if not "treating" yourself to– a new mixer, new wooden spoons, and even some cute cookie cutters. Before you decide what you want, take a quick look at these items.

ONCE YOU START YOUR BUSINESS

When you've made the decision to go into business, then you'll really want to take stock of what you have at home, of how old and dependable your current equipment is, and seriously updating it.

There are at least three good reasons for this. Depending on how old your appliances are, you may discover newer models use less electricity. Another excellent reason is that you won't have to worry about an appliance shutting down in the middle of a batch and the series of inconveniences that could cause. Best case scenario in this example is the inconvenience of having to temporarily stop everything with enough time to fix the problem and later continuing making treats that do not need to be shipped out just yet.

Worst case scenario, the production of treats come to a grinding halt, and you're at risk of missing a delivery date. Trust me, having something very close to that happen to me I must tell you; this is not a comfortable situation to find yourself in.

Depending on how old your equipment is, you'll also discover with new larger and easy-to-use appliances can make your baking so much easier.

WHAT TYPE OF EQUIPMENT

You could, if you had it, spend a fortune on the cutest equipment in the way of cookie cutters, molds, and even rolling pins. But before I outline a few of these things, there are two pieces of equipment that, while not every decorative, are instead extremely durable and certainly worth looking into. Remember, you'll soon need something like these main pieces as your business grows.

The first is a commercial bowl lift stand mixer. I finally broke down and bought one, and my only regret was not having bought it sooner. I won't recommend a brand to you, because you know what your favorite brands are and the ones you trust.

Mine is an eight-quart mixer and is easy to operate right from my kitchen counter. I strongly advise getting one with those characteristics, as it has facilitated the mixing portion of my business.

COMMERCIAL MIXER

Again, I wasn't even sure when I first launched my pet bakery that I needed this. Today, I couldn't imagine baking without it. The one I have has a half-gallon capacity with a commercial-grade motor, so you shouldn't have to worry about the amount of food you place in it.

The unexpected benefit with the blender, though, was that it can sit on my kitchen counter taking up a minimum of space.

ETCHED ROLLING PIN

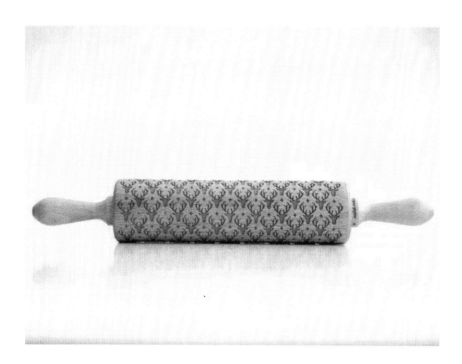

I found this wonderful rolling pin that has indents of dog-related decorations. This is not a mandated piece of equipment, but it may be the one thing that makes your products stand out from others in your region.

I roll out the dough for my dog treats using a regular flat rolling pin until I get the dough to the thickness I need. Then I do a once-over with this decorative roll so that when I cut the treats, they'll have random dog-related shapes on the top.

FOOD CONTAINERS WITH LIDS

You'll probably only need one of these food containers, to begin with, but as you continue in your endeavor and find your company growing, you'll need to add more. I personally like the eight-quart size and a Snap-On lid.

PASTRY CUTTER

Okay, you probably know this tool better as a pizza cutter. You'll need at least one of these. Along those lines, not too long ago I stumbled across an amazing device: a six-wheel pastry cutter.

Why? Because when you have many rectangular or diamond-shaped cookies or treats to cut, it'll save you time. Just be patient with it; there's definitely a learning curve when using it.

Before we start a discussion about my favorite piece of equipment– cookie cutters– here is a list of other pieces of equipment you'll eventually discover convenient, if not essential, as your pet bakery business grows.

COOKIE PRESS

This is essential if you plan on making spritz cookies at some point.

COOKIE SHEETS

You may also call these baking sheets. You've probably already figured this out. Just a hint: you may have one or two for your home. But as your business grows, you'll find the benefits of having several. Of course, your oven can only hold a finite number, but if you could have more than one or two ready to put in as soon as those in the oven are complete, your baking will go a lot faster.

In many ways, you'll be a one-person cookie assembly line to begin. Anything you can do to make you a more efficient baker will help. Before you know it, you'll be your own time-management expert.

DECORATING BAG

This piece of equipment comes in as part of a set. The bag should come with several different heads for a variety of decorative motifs. You may also want to consider using a disposable decorating bag, which eliminates the cleaning stage; when you're done with one bag, you'll just toss it.

DOUBLE BOILER

While not necessary, it does come in as a wonderful alternative to the microwave when you melt carob or yogurt coating. I prefer using a double boiler when melting these ingredients because there's a lesser chance of burning the items.

LARGE CUTTING OR PASTRY BOARD

This a much better way to roll out your dough and go a long way to keeping your kitchen table free of knife nicks.

CAKE PANS. MUFFIN PANS

If your thoughts zoom to round pans, it's time to adapt your thoughts to all kind of shapes and sizes. Start by looking on the internet. You'll find some of the most appropriate shapes and sizes for your business. One of my favorites that I find I use over and over again is a dog bone shaped cake pan. I get plenty of requests for this one for the birthday parties of many dogs.

When you move into your retail space

One of the benefits of working at home is not needing to buy a second set of equipment for the brick and mortar shop. While you work at home, you can always add to your needs as you grow. The moment you open the front doors of your retail shop to customers, you'll need to be fully stocked on all of your equipment.

COOKIE CUTTERS

One of the most useful pieces of specialty equipment that is well worth the price consists of cookie cutters.

Not just any cookie cutter, though. Whether they're in the shape of the stereotypical dog bone, dog houses, or the dogs themselves, any dog-related cookie cutter is just about guaranteed to be a big hit with pet owners.

One caveat before we go any further. I try not to use cutters with small ends that can easily break off in transit, or even when you're trying to wrap them. I'm specifically talking about the tails of the biscuits in the shapes of dogs.

If you take a good look at them, you'll see exactly what I mean. Of course, when you give them to your pets, you may not be as concerned. When you give them as gifts and especially when you sell them, you want each and every treat to be perfect. You just can't be selling doggie treats with broken tails to the public.

I try to stay with cutters with no small segments. Having said that, I know that dog-themed cutters are sold in all shapes and sizes. If your budget isn't large to start, then your best bet is to buy sets that come in approximately six to eight different sizes.

If you're making treats for the larger dog, then you want to make them from the largest cookie cutters you have. Accordingly, if you're making treats for smaller dogs, you'll make the treats smaller.

If you end up with several steady customers with small dogs, you might even want to invest in a set of mini-dog cookie cutters.

Here's a quick, creative idea. Why not give dog-themed cookie cutters to your friends who love dogs? Even if they don't do much baking, they won't resist using these.

Another creative idea is to hold a focus group or even just a party and make the human cookies out of the dog-themed shapes, and from there you can think of all sorts of other clever ideas.

Aside from dog bones and dog shapes, there are many different shapes that are perfect for your burgeoning business. Chew on this short list of ideas I snatched up as soon as I knew I was launching my own business.

- Dog houses
- Fire hydrants
- Cats
- Postal workers
- Squirrels

In addition to these, you'll want to stock up when you can on cutters with holiday-themed shapes. No need to buy special dog cutters for this. Any cutter you'd use for your cookies for the holidays would be perfect for the dog treats as well. Think Christmas, Easter, Hanukkah, Halloween.

When it comes to making treats for smaller dogs and other pets, you can easily find a mini-version of these, if not in your local craft store then online.

TIPS AND TECHNIQUES IN TREAT-MAKING

When a recipe calls for a certain shape cookie cutter, you're not going to destroy the recipe by using a different shape. In fact, that's the fastest and easiest way to put your own signature on the recipe.

Having trouble with the dough sticking to your cookie cutters? If this has become a habitual problem, rub some flour on the cutter, and this won't plague you.

CHAPTER 5: RECIPES

A few recipes to get the creative juices flowing...

Creativity– in any area of your life –is amazing. If you're a writer, you may be staring at a blank sheet of paper with no inspiration to write a single word. You don't even have a topic.

If you're a painter, the blank canvas is the largest step to overcome.

When you're a baker.

Wait, you didn't know that once you begin a bakery, you're wading into the creative arts? You are. It may be that your creative juices will need a bit of prodding, but once you search through all the recipes on the net, you'll soon get ideas of your own about creating new treats.

That's creativity.

We've included a few; you can find more on YouTube as well as a host of eBooks and print books. Once you find one you like, don't be afraid to tweak it to your liking. That's what baking and cooking are all about. Pet treats are no different in this aspect.

LADY'S OATS SNACKS

Ingredients

2 1/2 half cup rolled oats

1/2 teaspoon salt

1 egg

1/2 cup unsalted low-fat beef broth or chicken broth

Directions

Preheat oven to 325 degrees.

Mix 2 cups oats, salt, broth, and egg in a large bowl and combine well.

Once combined, mix the remaining oats and combine it all.

Pour this mixture on waxed paper and knead this for approximately three minutes. You'll want your dough to stand for about another three minutes to rest. During this time, the dough will get firmer. This is not only completely natural, but it's also exactly what you want.

Once the dough is firm, you need to spread it with a rolling pin into a thickness of about half an inch.

Cut these treats with a cookie cutter, then arrange them on a parchment-lined baking sheet.

Bake this for approximately 20 minutes. Once you remove these treats from the oven, allow them to cool completely

You can then either store these in an airtight container or a zipped storage bag, or you can freeze them for later as well.

One of the most satisfying aspects of baking dog treats is that some of the most delicious and nutritious ingredients for your dog come fresh from your refrigerator. I'm referring to the following recipe, which I named Lady's Poppin' Poppers. The not-so-secret ingredient you'll pet will love is the shredded carrots. The "poppin'" part of the treat? Cinnamon, which is included not only for taste but also to keep your pet's teeth healthy.

LADY'S POPPIN' POPPERS

Ingredients

1 ½ cup whole grain flour

½ cup shredded carrots

1 egg

½ tablespoon cinnamon powder

4 tablespoons bacon fat

Directions:

Preheat the oven to 350 degrees.

You'll want to prepare yourself for these ingredients by having two cookie sheets available lined with parchment paper.

Mix the carrots, cinnamon, egg, and bacon evenly in a bowl.

Add the flour and knead the resulting mixture for a few minutes.

Roll the dough to about ¼ inch thick. Cut the biscuits to a size of your choosing, depending on the dogs who will be eating them.

Bake for 15 minutes or until golden brown.

HEART-Y BEEF JERKY

Your dog will love this jerky because it's healthy and amazingly simple to make. This is one of my customers' favorite treats.

Ingredients:

1 beef heart

Directions:

You'll want to freeze the heart, so it's easier to slice. You'll slice the heart into strips approximately half-inch thick and one-inch in length

If you have a dehydrator, then you can pop the strips into it at 150 Fahrenheit for about 20 hours. If you don't have a dehydrator, then you can place the strips in your oven on the lowest setting for about the same amount of time.

Then place these slices on a parchment-covered baking sheet and allow it to dry overnight in the oven. You'll want to keep the oven door propped open some during this period.

It only makes sense. We, humans, go crazy over bacon. Some restaurants sell bacon milkshakes, for example. So, a peanut butter, banana, and bacon bite treat for your pup seems not only natural, but also sounds good to many humans as well.

Ingredients

1 cup whole grain flour

2 thick slices of bacon—not smoked

1 ripe banana (about 1/3 cup when mashed)

3 tablespoons peanut butter

Directions:

Preheat oven to 350 degrees Fahrenheit.

Fry bacon until it's crispy.

After the bacon is cooled, break it into smaller pieces.

In a small bowl, mash the banana with a fork and then fold in the peanut butter.

Add the flour next. Mix the resulting mixture gently.
Then you can add the bacon bits at the end.
Stir them into the dough until they are evenly
distributed shape dough into balls. If you like to keep
all treats about the same size, use a tablespoon.

Place each treat on a parchment-lined cookie sheet
about two inches separate from one another.
Bake for about 15 minutes or until golden brown.

DOGGIE-OHS!

Let's face it. While the final word on the success of a
treat comes from Fido or Lady, you still have to
market to their owners. I've found that this "cookie"
does both. Pet owners go crazy just seeing that the
cookie looks so close to your childhood favorites,
Oreos. But your dog— and your customers' pet— will
love the taste.

Ingredients for the cookie sandwich portion:

2 cups whole wheat flour
4 tablespoons carob powder
2 eggs

2 tablespoons vegetable oil

Ingredients for the crème filling:

5 tablespoons cream cheese

Preheat oven to 350 degrees Fahrenheit

Mix the eggs and oil in a small bowl. Separately mix the carob powder with flour. Then mix both your dry and wet ingredients together. You want the dough to be pliable once you're done mixing. If the dough is too runny, add flour, and if the dough appears too dry, add a bit of water to the mixture.

Next, roll the dough to ¼-thickness. Cut the cookies with a round cookie cutter.

You'll bake these for 20 minutes and allow them to cool completely.

Once cooled, spread cream cheese over one cookie and top the treat with a second cookie.

Lady's Refreshing Breath Mint

Ingredients:

- ½ cups whole grain flour
- ½ cups rice flour
- 2 teaspoons cinnamon
- ½ cup fresh chopped mint
- ½ cup chopped fresh parsley
- ¾ vegetable stock
- 2 cups whole wheat flour

Directions:

Preheat oven to 350 degrees Fahrenheit

Blend stock and fresh herbs until the stock turns into a thick green liquid.

Mix the dry ingredients, both segments of the flour in the ingredient list, and the cinnamon.

Mix the liquid with the dry ingredients.

Shape this dough into a long stick. Cut it into approximately 5-inch segments and allow them to dry for a day or so. Once they've dried, you can store them in an air-tight container.

CHAPTER 6: DO YOU HAVE WHAT IT TAKES TO BUILD A PET BAKERY BUSINESS?

I recently delivered an order of dog treats to a small local pet shop. The manager of the store took his order then commented, "It must be an ideal life," and added before I could answer, "All you have to do all day long is make dog treats. What an easy way to make money. Nothing like how a real entrepreneur works all day."

I took a deep breath, nodded, and made a quick exit. I didn't feel like explaining my time to him.
I mention this because he isn't the first person to tell me my day must be filled with baking dog treats. If the main reason you want to open a pet bakery is to spend your days baking, then my guess is your business isn't going to last very long– and it sounds like you'll have a great deal of treats leftover.

Believe it or not, more individuals than I care to count use their love of baking as the number one reason why they want to start a dog bakery.

While you certainly will find yourself making plenty of treats, including birthday cakes, "power bars," and much more, you also have more responsibilities. And you'd better be ready to wear several different hats at one time, especially if you launch your pet bakery from home.

The following chapter details what characteristics are needed to be wildly successful and outrageously happy in this business.

First and foremost, don't start a dog bakery business if you have any doubts at all about what you want to do. It's fine to be mulling it over before you make up your mind. That's called wise decision-making. But once you decide that this is the business for you, then you have to throw your full commitment to it. You can't decide in the middle of all your plans that you're having doubts about your degree of dedication to the process.

This is called intent. You have to form an intention in your mind that no amount of people telling you you're making "the biggest mistake of your life" could ever shake your belief in your decision.

If you have laser intention, then it will be without a doubt a labor of love. What you should consider when those naysayers are reminding you about the mistake they think you are about to make, you have to flip that question around and ask yourself, "Will not starting this business be the biggest mistake of my life? Will it become one of my biggest regrets?"

And only you can answer that.

GOAL-ORIENTED

Even before you open the doors of your pet bakery or go live on your website, you'll learn how much this part of your life is all about setting goals. Setting goals and keeping goals, specifically.

Have you noticed that when you set a personal goal, it's all too easy to push it out of the way simply because something "more important" has come up. No, when you've dedicated your day or portions of your day to this start-up business, there is nothing more important than what you're doing. You can't postpone or procrastinate working on your goals, for example.

You must be pig-headed, as they say— you need to be all about meeting these goals. Of course, you need to be flexible because there always be some hurdle thrown at you that may trip you up. But if that's the case, you rework your timeline, make yourself another goal, and get on with your start-up, or gaining customers, or even filling orders.

THE CHARACTERISTICS OF A HIGHLY SUCCESSFUL ENTREPRENEUR

Ever since I was a child, I was always enamored with the word entrepreneur. First, it sounded foreign and exotic to me. And you know, in its own special way, it really is exotic. Let's face it, few individuals have what it takes to walk away from their day job, or not even consider a day job, and rely– especially at the beginning– on themselves for their daily income.

Unfortunately, you can scour Amazon all day long, or walk through the Barnes and Nobles bookstores for hours, and you'll never find the definite blueprint of how to ensure your 100 percent success in this area. That's because there is none. Each individual is unique and comes to their projects with their own set of reasons and, in many cases, intuitive characteristics because of his or her passion for his or her project.

But there are a few traits that all entrepreneurs have in common. And while matching your personality and intentions up against these are no guarantee of success, they will give you a big picture to compare your characteristics to.

GOAL ORIENTED

There's no doubt about it; entrepreneurs are dedicated to setting and meeting goals with the aim of making their business dream a reality. That means, as we've said earlier in this chapter, there is no hurdle too large to stop them from achieving their goals.

Where others see boulders in the path before them, the entrepreneur sees an opportunity to work around and, in the process, learn how to handle the next one.

STRATEGIC THINKERS

You may reserve this type of language for four-star generals or military types. The truth of the matter is that the best entrepreneurs are strategic thinkers.

What I mean is that they know in their minds what their "end game" is; in this case, the best pet bakery they could manifest. Along the way, strategic thinkers all know how they plan to achieve this final goal.

The most amazing entrepreneurs are also amazingly committed to their business. Not easily discouraged, they see failure from a vastly different perspective from the average person. The heart of the matter is that individuals with these characteristics seem to have blinders on when it comes to failure. Where many individuals see failure, these people see an opportunity for future success.

Any trip up along the way, any mistake doesn't diminish their enthusiasm, but only enhances it.

HANDS-ON

Don't get me wrong. A business person reviewing his or her launch and startup will certainly delegate specific tasks to others. But they are also extremely and enthusiastically hands-on. If there's an aspect of the business they believe they have the best knowledge of, they won't hesitate to jump right in and do so.

If you ask them about this, a hands-on person will probably tell you that they see themselves as "doers", not thinkers.

In fact, entrepreneurs, for the most part, view their business— whether it's a dog bakery business or an online informational business— as an extension of themselves.

FLOURISH ON UNCERTAINTY

Waking up in the morning and not knowing what awaits them makes them all the more enthusiastic about getting down to business. That doesn't mean they invite chaos, but they don't let the diversity of their job allow them to doubt the direction they've taken is nothing but right.

The corollary to this statement is that the true entrepreneur remains calm in the face of unexpected events thrown at his or her plans. He or she remains calm throughout all possible situations. This person doesn't panic and acts like Chicken Little in the fable where the main character scatters and tells everyone who will listen that the sky is falling after a misunderstanding.

That's because the individual who flourishes on uncertainty knows that the sky isn't falling and every situation, however gloomy it may appear, will often have a silver lining and bring an even brighter, larger, and more lucrative opportunity.

THEY SEARCH FOR OPPORTUNITIES

Speaking of opportunities, the highly successful entrepreneur will actually search out for bigger and better opportunities. He or she isn't normally satisfied with the status quo, not when something can be improved. Any idea can be expanded, and every day is seen as the perfect chance for another day of creativity.

RISK TAKER

An entrepreneur is willing and eager to take risks. That's because, unlike some individuals, they never question whether the act will succeed. They don't have to; they know intuitively it will.

Here's a hint of why they know: they won't let the opportunity slip out of their hands before they have achieved it. They aren't arrogant, but rather confident, and with that confidence, the universe will provide them with the success they already see.

LISTEN AND LEARN

With all the actions they take, with all the hands-on experience they gain, they have one extra perhaps counterintuitive skill: they listen to others and learn from them. While they have their goals aligned and their vision fresh in their minds, they are more than willing to listen to other viewpoints and carefully take them into account.

The entrepreneur knows that every project is buttressed by the input of others. That every opportunity is enhanced when he considers the advice of others.

PEOPLE SKILLS

You might think someone, as driven as a entrepreneur, might be lacking social graces. You need to revise that image a bit actually because studies show that just the opposite is true. The most successful business owners usually have the best ability to communicate and are highly adept at working with others.

This particular characteristic is essential regarding their ability to sell their products to their customers.

But that's not the only place where this characteristic is required. These highly developed people skills are used to encourage, motivate, and inspire those around them. Of course, not every business owner is a Steve Jobs, the late CEO of Apple. But as you develop a sphere of influence of your own, you'll soon see and be amazed at what a great motivator you can become.

CREATIVITY

Every highly successful entrepreneur is highly creative. While some people limit creativity to drawing or writing, the word covers a much wider range of abilities and uses than one would originally expect.

Just the idea that they can see and recognize an opportunity for a new product or project where others see nothing but a hurdle shows their creativity. Their ability to manifest that concept into reality is yet another illustration of their inherent creativity.

PASSIONATE ABOUT THEIR WORK

Whether they're working on their first business or the fifth in the line of new products, the highly successful entrepreneur remains passionate about what they are doing, so they find it easy to put the hours and work into their business.

In fact, because of this overriding passion, nothing that they do when it comes to their business is considered work. They may call it a labor of love, but even that isn't right. Many times, when an entrepreneur invests time into their business, they are really just in the zone; when such a person is fully in the moment, there is no work, no effort. Just doing.

Let's be honest, not every successful entrepreneur has every single one of these traits. Some are better at breaking through barriers that have the potential to cause others to pause and question their course. Some business owners are more adept at people skills than at creativity.

But when you look at this list, there are only two things to keep in mind. How closely you really do match any of these abilities, and how you intend to improve them. This is because the more you sharpen these characteristics, the more affluent your dog bakery will become.

However, when you surround yourself with like-minded individuals who have some of the traits you aren't as strong at, then you can be sure your business will be highly successful itself.

CHAPTER 7: BUILDING A BRIDGE FROM HOBBY TO BUSINESS

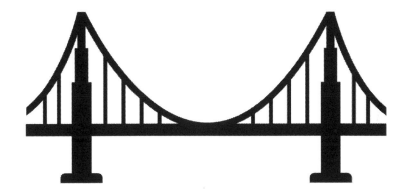

As you're bridging that move from hobbyist to serious pet bakery owner, you'll need to take a bite out of several of these choices, not the least at which is the best direction in which to start.

Do you start your business from your home initially, or are you going to rent a retail building? Of course, there are advantages and disadvantages to each. While many individuals instinctively choose to launch from their homes, many jump right in with a physical presence in a local neighborhood.

For example, if you choose the retail path, you will certainly have the opportunity to reach more people far more quickly than the home start-up option. That's a plus. You have the chance of getting total strangers to walk in who just happen to be walking by and stop in on impulse. And while you may expect them to be pet owners, some of them may not be.

They may have relatives or friends who have pets and will buy something for their pets on impulse simple on how you've presented your products.

Starting at Home

I started my business from home. I had to tell you part of the reason was that I was still skeptical that a pet bakery as a separate establishment would make money. So, for me, I was making decisions that would increase the odds of me succeeding wildly. So far, it's working.

But there are other benefits to starting your business from home.

START-UP COSTS ARE LOWER

With lower launch costs, you can dig in and concentrate on making money faster than if you opened a brick and mortar pet bakery. It may take years before you break even financially with a retail pet bakery. When you work from home, the profits may be small to start, but they will eventually begin to flow in. Once they flowed in, I re-routed much of that back into the business.

ALLOWED ME TO CONCENTRATE ON AN ONLINE PRESENCE

Without the worry of building a local business, I had the time and energy to spend on making a great impression online. My reasoning was simple. For the long-term, I knew that I was creating a large, loyal following. I don't have to depend on variables out of my control to have a good sales day. There are always individuals walking through my internet neighborhood, so to say.

What's even better, the longer I'm an online seller, the more customers I get. I will tell you making your presence on the web doesn't happen overnight, but if you stick with it, you'll find that market you're looking for.

OTHER BENEFITS

As a home start-up business, my bakery can explore other sometimes lucrative options for my presence elsewhere. What do I mean by this? I mean that I can plan my weekends to take my treats to dog shows, sell them at craft shows, and place them for consignment sales at small retail stores that cater to dog services.

Here's something else to chew on. I was able to cut a deal with a local groomer so that he would not only take my treats on a consignment basis but also offer a complimentary one to his customers for their dog's good behavior at the groomer's. I can't tell you how many loyal customers I have right now because of that special relationship.

This strategy works for me because the target market for gourmet, organic treats is quite varied. I knew there was a wide customer base for items from a pet bakery, I just never realized the extent of the diversity before starting my business.

Of course, the one item that ties all these customers together are the dogs. But my customers include those individuals who themselves only eat organic foods, and who by extension believe it would be a good idea for their pets to have an organic diet as well.

I have individuals as customers who have been lifelong dog breeders whose success depends on the shiny coats and other physical attributes the dogs may have. I also have customers who are middle-age persons, mostly empty nesters who filled that nest with their pets and are therefore willing to give their furry friends extravagant treats.

Then there are younger customers who have decided to wait for a better time to have children, and follow the same logic when it comes to feeding their dogs or cats better foods than the standard commercially-bought items.

When you think about it, working from home gives you the opportunity to find customers everywhere, starting with your own online presence.

As you consider the establishments you approach to help disburse your treats, don't forget a few more of the obvious ones such as dog learning centers, health food stores for humans, and doggy daycare centers.

THE DISADVANTAGES

Let's face it, as much as we'd love to claim it was so; it isn't: gourmet pet treats aren't in demand evenly across the nation. If you're stuck in a brick and mortar store, you may have a limited market.

You must be cognizant of specific rules and regulations of your local agencies, starting with your local health department. Find out what rules you need to get up to speed to. Are there local permits you need to get as a retail bakery– even one for pets?

If you decide to start a retail business, think about the costs involved in either purchasing or renting a space, along with the potential up-keep of the structure.

And we haven't even factored in expenses the decoration used in order to create a welcoming and clever theme.

Of course, you may be tempted to purchase a franchise. You should know up front that this is typically one of the most expenses moves you can make. On the plus side, you will have a nationally or regionally recognized name to draw customers closer.

On the more practical level, opening a retail bakery means buying an entire set of equipment for producing the treats. When you start at home, you can use much of the same utensils and appliances found in your home. Dog food treats don't require much in the way of special equipment.

Developing and Refining Your Products

At the same time, you're considering what sources you'd like to sell your products to, start thinking about your product line. In addition to treats, what else do you plan to sell? To answer this question, you may want to research some. You'll need to know what's trending in treats at the moment, as well as how pet owners are pampering their pets.

Consider this: more pet owners than ever before are throwing their pets birthday parties, with a birthday cake and all. Not only that, but you'll see some photos of parties in which the dogs are the true guests and are sitting at the kitchen table and look as if they know the full intent of what they're doing.

You may want to try baking a birthday cake for a pet party as part of developing this as a possible offering.

When you're testing ideas, you could rely on family and friends. I've always done this, but there was always a small voice in the back of my mind that told me they were merely being kind. What I truly wanted was constructive criticism, the good suggestions, even ways of improving what I'm currently baking.

There's a lot to be said for holding focus groups with individuals you only know casually or not at all. You can do this in many ways if you don't feel like addressing six to eight complete strangers in a meeting– I can understand how that can be daunting.

But there are other ways to do this. Some of these may be considered continuous improvements. This is something I do on a regular basis: when a craft show is announced, I immediately rent a table. Not only do I plan to fill the table with my tried, true, and successful products, but if I haven't had time prior to this to develop a few new products, I do so immediately.

I don't know about your area, but craft show attendees love to bring their dogs with them, which is why I bring a few of these untested products with me. If the craft attendee and his pet are at the table, I hand a treat to the owner and explain what I'm doing. I ask him if it wouldn't spoil any of his dog's meals and if the owner would let his pup have it now. Through this way, I can get the dog's first reaction to it.

In the meantime, I'm also asking questions of my potential customer– questions about packaging, pricing, what their preference is when it comes to ingredients. I ask them if they have any specific ingredients they want to see in the treats. When I'm done asking questions, I give them a small sample of my products packaged as a thank you gift for being patient and helping me gain insight.

This strategy can be used anywhere from swap meets to flea markets. You can even visit dog shows using this method.

You may also want to ask how your prices stand up to others. Not everyone will be comfortable answering this question, but if you do find someone who is, it could possibly be some of your most valuable part of your survey.

If potential customers suggest anything, don't dismiss their comments out of hand. Give serious thought to them, especially if more than one individual suggests the same thing.

WHERE ARE YOUR BEST OUTLETS WHEN BUYING SUPPLIES?

Your search should start on the internet, mostly because unless you're selling a large number of treats, you probably won't be able to buy anything in bulk. That means your best bet is the internet, which can cut you the best deal.

This is not to say you shouldn't check out local and regional retailers. If there are main differences between online businesses and local retailers, you may want to choose local. When at all possible, you should also shop in person instead of mail order. You may feel as if you don't have time. But you'll find the benefits of naturally networking this way are invaluable.

Finally, as you continue on with your journey toward entrepreneurship, you'll meet more pet bakery owners. As you get to know them better, you'll feel more comfortable asking them where they get their supplies– any specialized flours, themed cookie cutters, even molds for dog treats.

WHAT SHOULD I CHARGE FOR MY PRODUCTS?

That's an excellent question. Not only do you have to take into account the cost of your supplies, but also of your time. I'll be honest with you. When I first began my business, I'm pretty sure I failed to factor in the amount of time and effort I put in the form of labor into the prices.

To be honest, I really didn't care at that point. I was thrilled to be running my own business. Do I recommend you do that? No, no, no! Make sure– regardless how small it may seem– you take into account at least some of the time you invest in your business. If nothing else, it's a great habit to get into. If you can do this know then you don't have to worry about it later, since paying yourself will become second nature.

When pricing the dog treats, cakes, and other bakery items, you'll feel pressure— mostly from yourself— to undercut all other bakery owners. I even know your logic. If you can price your products as the least expensive, then you can entice customers to try your product and . . . voilà!. . dogs love your product, they're the least expensive, and you'll have an immediate large and loyal customer base.

It would be great if the business world worked that way. This may surprise you, but if you undercut your competitors' prices, you run into several problems. First, customers will question why your product is so cheap if there's such a wide gap between prices. If they're already dog bakery customers, then they're used to paying a certain general price. If they find an item that seems out of their norm for paying, they will most likely get suspicious because they're pleased with the quality they're already paying for.

They immediately might think that the products you are offering are not up to the quality they're used to buying.

But not only that, if you price your products too low, you may unwittingly be pricing yourself out of business. I'm sure you already know this intuitively, but it bears reminding you, correct product pricing can make the difference between you being wildly successful or giving up and abandoning your business.

Having said that, I'm going to run through the proper way to price your products. This was one area in which I was clueless. Had I known some of these ideas before I even started, I may have been making money a bit sooner.

PRIMER ON PRICING

Pricing your products to make sure they're fair to both your customers and yourself really isn't that difficult at all as long as you follow a few easy guidelines.

DETERMINE THE COST OF YOUR INGREDIENTS

What you're doing here basically is taking all the ingredients in this particular treat and keep track of what they cost you. For example, if the flour is in the treat you're pricing, and you paid $3.50 for the last 5-pound bag, write it down.

From here, you determine the number of "units" this bag of flour contains. This requires a bit of math knowledge and a trusty calculator by your side. You will discover that there are 3.5 cups of flour in one pound of flour. This means that there are 17.5 cups of flour in a 5-pound bag.

Your next step is to divide the total number of cups in the bag, the 17.5 cups into the total cost of the five-pound bag. When you calculate this, you learn that a cup of flour costs you approximately 20 cents a cup. By extension, if you only used a half a cup, then can easily see that it your cost is 10 cents for half a cup.

Now, determine how much flour was used in your package of treats, and continue doing this for every ingredient in your product. Once you've done this, create a chart that itemizes all the ingredients along with the top.

I organize mine this way.

Ingredient	Unit	Cost
This is where you'll detail every ingredient used in the baking of a product	This column lists the actual amounts you use. For example, the flour which we've already used as an example would be broken down into smaller and smaller units.	In this column, you'll determine the cost of these units. It's exactly what we have written above but in a handy chart form. In this way, I find I don't have to calculate and recalculate my costs. Not, at least, until the cost of flour changes.
Unbleached flour	1 cup	$.20
Unbleached flour	½ cup	$.10
Unbleached flour	¼ cup	$.05

Whole wheat flour	1 cup	
Whole wheat flour	½ cup	
Whole wheat flour	¼ cup	

You can get a clear enough of an idea of what my finished chart looks like when all the ingredients for the products are filled in. Include even the ingredients that appear to be small and inconsequential on the surface, like salt, baking powder, or any spices you may have used.

Yes, the first time you create this chart, it's likely to be tedious. But you can see, even at a casual glance that it's going to save you much time in the long run.

Once you've created this chart, you'll make another one. This one deals with your recipes. That's the bad news. The good news is that you'll only have to make this chart once. You should not only have these charts carefully filed in your computer, but you may also want print them out and slip them in a clear sheet protector for a three-ring notebook. In the following chart, I'll show you how easy it is to make the recipe chart. Pull out your recipes, the ones for treats you've already made. Again, I'll use one of my recipes to illustrate how easy it is to do.

I have a recipe I call Lady's Chicken Treats. I started calculating my cost of production by performing the following steps. This is exactly what you'll replicate with each of your recipes.

1. List the ingredients

Once you've done this, then you can figure out the cost, like we did in the previous paragraphs.

2. Total the costs

Calculate the cost for a batch of Lady's Chicken Treats. You need to know how many treats are in a batch. For the most part, I get approximately three dozen treats out of one batch. That's 36 treats.

3. Calculate the cost for one treat

For me, one batch of these treats cost me, in total, $24.84 to make. If you take that number and divide it by the chicken treats in a batch, you see that one treat costs about $0.69. Let's make this clear: one treat costs me $0.69. If I sell those treats for anything less, I'd be losing money immediately.

But wait. Once you know what it costs to make, you can calculate many other aspects of your pricing philosophy, all with the goal of maximizing your profits.

Now we're going to check out how much money you have invested in the packaging of these treats. I package Lady's Chicken's Treats in a cellophane bakery bag; One bag costs me $.40. I sell the treats in packages of six.

Right now, it appears that my costs for a package of six of these treats now stand at $0.814. That's the addition of the costs of six treats $0.414 plus $0.40 for the packaging. I round this up to $0.82.

Next, I'm going to estimate my expenses for labor and overhead. Since I work from home, this is easy and doesn't really add that much to the cost. I chose to put the cost of those treats at $2.00.

USING MARKET RESEARCH IN PRICING

You may think you're done pricing your product. Certainly, when I launched my business, I considered myself done. Until that is, I learned how to use market research to see how my prices held up against the "competition."

I began haunting pet bakeries in my area, browsed the topic online, and walked around flea markets, swaps, and any other location I could find the sale of similar treats. I try as much as possible to keep my prices in similar price ranges.

Now that you've figured your costs, set a price, and verified you're in the ballpark by checking other bakeries and home-sellers, you might consider yourself done and ready to sell them.

You're almost ready. But you still have one more step. What do you do if you discover a bakery selling a treat similar in size to Lady's Chicken Treats?

These treats sell well for the bakery at a price of $0.75 each.

You're confident, after all, that your costs are well below that. Despite that, you make the decision to change the price per individual treat at $0.75. That means you now charge a package of six treats for $4.50 a bag. Remember, the cost to you is only $2.00.

Let's extrapolate this a bit. If you remember, I said I could make six bags of treats from one batch. Now you've just increased your profit to $15.00 when you sell the entire batch of treats. Not bad for one batch.

ALL THE STEPS WORK TOGETHER

Now you have seen how all these steps work together, not unlike a fine orchestra. Your initial pricing and suggested profit were good. But as you added layers to your initial findings, you have just created a greater profit for you while not feeling like you're overcharging your customers.

And you can see how it's important to go through this routine for every recipe, every product you sell.

CHAPTER 8: MARKETING

Marketing. It's easier than you think. There seems to be far too many people today writing about all the nuances of marketing. You already realize I'm sure, that there are certain fundamental acts you should take. You know you'll need business cards and a website.

In this chapter, I'm detailing the marketing tools I used that seemed to work best. Keep in mind that there are plenty of paths to successful marketing. But there are a few steps that work best for the pet bakery business. Those are the ones we're going to talk about now.

FREE SAMPLES

This technique probably works best with all food marketing, but it does so particularly well for me. Some of my friends and many family members thought I was crazy at first. They told me not to give so many samples. The goal, they told me, was to have people buy the treats.

I agreed with the end game, but I stood my ground. And yes, there were times when it felt as if I were giving away more samples than selling them, which I was, but that didn't bother me. I knew that the best marketing tool was word of mouth. So I set out to create a bit of word of mouth.

HOW DID I DO THIS?

I picked my favorite treat at the time, wrapped it up carefully, so it looked attractive, made sure it had all my business information and contact information on it. I chose first to gift these to dog groomers to give to their customers as gifts.

I also searched all the dog-related businesses like doggie daycare and dog obedience schools. During this process, I discovered that there were several breeders in the area and I delivered my treats to these business owners themselves for their own use and for their customers. I also have no doubt that this method took my dog treats to areas I never would have thought to go. I can't I tell you how many people I never met called me after that to place orders.

But more than that, I posted business cards on every grocery store bulletin board and any big box chains in the hopes that even remotely dealt in any dog products.

MAKE A PHYSICAL PRESENCE IN THE AREA

At the same time, I researched all the dog shows and other related events I could find in my area. If there were tables for rent for vendors, I was there. This not only proved to be an effective and lucrative marketing strategy, but it also became an invaluable networking.

But all in all, I had to admit that one of the very best places to give free samples and place your business cards if you can is at the local veterinarian office. I was fortunate enough to have two in the small city I lived in and several not very far away. All agreed to give them away, and several vets immediately asked for several small packages they could sell.

I can't say that I began making sales from these actions overnight; all of these actions worked together over time to create a solid foundation for what's turning out to be a profitable business.

RETURN CUSTOMERS

Wow! Before I knew it, my pet bakery was off and running smoothly. Every one of my new customers seemed genuinely satisfied with my products. But I knew I still had to devise a long-term marketing plan that could turn those first and even second-time customers into long-time regulars.

The best way to do that, I decided, was to continually update my "menu." I did this for two reasons– one being the people customer and the second being the pet customer. If you're like me, there are just sometimes when buying the same product over and over again gets old. Sometimes faster than you could believe

As you have probably guessed, you can't set up a store or an online presence and expect customers to come flocking to you without some type of marketing. You have to let them know that your business has opened, and you have to give them a reason to visit you.

If you really think about it, that's the entire purpose of marketing and advertising. That, in effect, is what we've been discussing. Along those lines, we can't talk enough about where to find your new customers. The key is to remember that you just can't randomly choose households to target. It's imperative you know where you can find your future customers.

For example, one of the best places to find future customers is online. Some of you may think of this as a no-brainer, but for others, it could be a revelation. You've set up a website; perhaps now it's time to create a blog that talks about dog health, treats or any other topic related to pets.

One of the first laws of good salesmanship is that it's easier to sell to a friend than a stranger. Once you start blogging, perhaps even keep an email list, and periodically give them an update of what you're doing, more customers are bound to get curious and try some of your goods. How about when it comes to new products?

You can also use your blog and your email list to inform them of new research in pet nutrition or new pet-related trends.

This tip works for so many aspects of your business.

This is a subject we talked about in the startup of your business. But it's also an awesome marketing tool: create products that are unique to your business. It's a product that you and no one else in your area sells, for example. I started with one product. Since I didn't know how well it would sell, I studied its sales carefully. It didn't take me long to realize that it was an instant hit and the fact was it became a great marketing tool.

Today I have a line of a half dozen or so products which I call Lady's Signature's Line and then a small graphic of a paw. When I introduce a new product in the signature line, I make sure my email list has a heads up before any other customers have a chance to buy them.

Then I make an announcement on my website and sell these new goods to all my other customers. Doing this, by the way, gives your customers a good reason to enroll on your list. You may also want to call the list something that connotes that they are special customers.

Don't be afraid to give those names on your email list exposure to special price discounts.

This is just a small portion of the marketing ideas available to you. When you're mind mapping your ideas, you're limited only by your imagination. Don't be afraid to try any idea that sounds good to you. If it doesn't work, you can always start over again with another idea.

Right now, it's probably a good time to let some of those ideas in your mind simmer while we talk about the legal aspects of launching a pet bakery business.

CHAPTER 10: LEGALLY SPEAKING
BUSINESS PLAN

You have many ideas rolling around in your head right about now, from the name of your business, to your menu, to whether your debut bakery will be in your home, online, or with a ribbon-cutting ceremony of a neighborhood bakery retail store.

If you're like me, until I firmly put my foot down, I flirted with them all. Ultimately, I decided to work from home, which afforded me the opportunity to build a website for a powerful online presence when I was ready.

In the meantime, the website was a great way for my customers to contact me, reorder, and do just about anything else. My home business kept me busy and making money. As I grew more adept at my business, I noticed my website was beginning to attract more customers.

Even though I wasn't planning for a brick and mortar bakery for a while, I included it my eventual roadmap, just in case. In this way, when the time came to show a lender how I intended to get there from here, it would already be done on paper. Then I could read it occasionally, and more often when I need a boost when I feel as if I'm just spinning my wheels.

Don't let these six words stop you:

It's only a pet bakery business.

What it really is a vital, lucrative niche market. And because of that, it deserves a well-thought-out business plan to keep you on track and to give you powerful, persuasive business presence should you decide you need to borrow money.

You may decide if you're not going to borrow money anytime soon, why you should even create one before you're fully in business. Many individuals– myself included before I did my research about starting a business– firmly believed a business plan had one and only one function: to give your lender an overall view of your future plan so he or she could decide if his or her money would be invested wisely.

The last thing a lender wants to hear is that they have loaned money to a business that within a year or so– before the loan has been fully repaid– has tanked. And the lender has no way of getting any of his money back by that point.

This chapter is a short summary of what a business plan is composed of and how it can not only help you attract a high-quality lender, but also provide you with a detailed road map of where you want to go.

Trust me, when you're in full swing of planning and running your business, you're consumed with short-term goals. Delivering the doggie birthday cake by 3:00 p.m. to the Jones', restocking the pet groomer who called this morning . . . well, you get the idea.

With a well-written detailed business plan, you can refer to how much you thought you'd grow at this stage and make any adjustments depending on how it compares to your new reality.

I know that the thought of writing what many see as a lengthy and somewhat boring document may appear to be a waste of time. But what I did and now urge you to do is to write it from your passion, and write it with the intent that this is your step-by-step blueprint for building your dream business.

Some hard-core business person may disagree with me. But I tell you this not only to keep you buoyed when your project runs into a hurdle. I'm telling you this because if you write it with enthusiasm and energy, your potential lender will feel it and have a feeling that their firm's money is in good hands.

There are normally six parts to any business plan. We'll quickly go through these step-by-step. What I'm presenting you is a broad outline, and it's up to you fill it with your statistics and plans and, of course, your enthusiasm.

MANAGEMENT SUMMARY

In this first section, you'll record who's responsible for managing your bakery as anybody you've designated as part of the management team. For the moment, this may just be you. If you decide, though, to open a retail store, you'll have to start thinking about a second in command and what type of qualities and experience you want this person to possess. Your lender at this stage wants to know who's in charge and whether they are qualified either by experience or by degree.

FINANCIAL ANALYSIS

The potential lender wants you to put on your prognosticator hat. You 'll need to estimate the operating costs of your business, including how much funding you'll need to run it at best.

Be honest in this area. This is your chance to ask for anything you want without restrictions. While you may not receive it all, chances are if the loan is approved, you'll have enough money to get off to a great start.

Remember, also use this for your wish list. You may want to refer to this plan, again and again, just to remind yourself of some of these small but vital steps that will make your business attractive to potential customers, and to make your ultimate dream come true.

APPENDICES AND EXHIBITS

You can use this section as you wish or as you need to, especially when it comes to data that backs and explains your decision. Among some of the documents, you'll want to be sure to include:

DEMOGRAPHIC RESEARCH

If you're going to open a retail store, this research should make it clear why you plan to put your pet bakery in a certain section of town. Demographics will also back your decision to decide what your ideal market is. Millennials? Baby Boomers?

You'll also want to indicate what their yearly incomes are. You certainly don't want to market to individuals who don't have the extra income to buy your dog treats on a regular basis.

STATISTICS

In this section, you'll want to talk about in as much detail as you can about your niche market in general, which in this case would be pet bakery. Data such as growth rate, increase in demands within the last several years, and even highly successful pet bakeries across the country is to be included.

Beyond that, feel free to show how dog ownership has grown and will continue growing, to reinforce the belief that the demand for products like yours will also increase.

PHOTOS

Don't be shy and certainly don't think you're wasting your lender's time by including photos of your products in your business plan. These graphics show that you take a professional approach and attitude to your bakery. They'll lift all doubt that you're only dabbling and that you're not only serious, but that you're good at it as well.

Show 'Em the Recipes

Well, not all of your recipes. But by all means, take a recipe or two that best represent certain categories of your overall menu. This could include a few dog treats, a cake for pets, even cupcakes. If you've developed a signature product, then by all means, you'll want to use your business journal to provide your lender that recipe and be sure to make it clear that your singular product sets you apart from the others.

That's an understated aim of this business plan: making your mark in the market.

Your Marketing Plan

You don't need to go into any large detail, but here again, your goal in this section is to show your would-be lender knows you understand the fundamentals of marketing your business. He or she will be interested in what kind of advertising you'd be doing, especially to gain initial customers. And of course, he or she also wants to know how to plan to make your initial customer a loyal, regular customer.

Don't panic if at this moment you haven't a clue how to conduct a marketing campaign— especially when it comes to a pet bakery. Later in this book, we talk about it to give you an idea about how easy it really is. By the time you're ready to create your business plan, you're more than willing to share your marketing plans with anyone who'll listen.

And, of course, your lender is also interested in learning your thoughts about how you'll attract new customers throughout your business career.

WHERE IS YOUR BAKERY?

If you haven't made it clear up to this point, now is a good as time as any to reveal the location for your business. Are you opening a retail pet bakery from an existing building? If so, what kind of neighborhood have you chosen and why?

Or are you planning to work out of your home and through the internet?

In this section, you'll want to explain your costs, whichever route you're planning on taking.

It's not gossip; it's research

Your lender really does want to know who you consider as your competitors and how you plan to compete them. Your potential lender needs to know you have researched them, what they offer, and how you're going to stand out from the crowd.

And the cost . . .

Don't forget to include perhaps the most important part of your pet bakery business plan: the amount of money you'd like to borrow in order to get your dream off the ground and running smoothly.

6 MUST DO'S FOR YOUR NEW START-UP

Here are the 6 must take steps for any new business startups, I've learned from experience and from talking to others in the industry that there are six specific things you need to do to get your new business off to a good start.

NAME YOUR BUSINESS

You need to get customers to distinguish your product from others in the same industry. This means you are going to need a business name; and not just any name. You want a short name that is easy to remember while also being catchy.
You need to make sure the name you choose isn't being used by any other company. If you want to know about business names you need to contact the Patent and Trade Mark Office.

One good way to search is by searching the name you picked on Google to see if anyone else is using it for the same purpose. My advice is if you find a good name, go ahead and buy the domain name of the name you just picked, this way in future if you ever want to grow, you can have a website under that name.

You can go to Godaddy.com or name.com or any other domain name seller's site and just type the name you picked; they will tell you if that name is available for purchase with.com or .net. Typically most domain names cost around $10/year which in my opinion is a great investment.

LICENSE YOUR BUSINESS

All businesses need proper licenses to operate. This shows that you are running a legal business. However, before you are allowed to license a business, you need to determine a structure for your business. If you know an accountant or an attorney, ask them to file a legal business entity (Like an LLC, S Corp or LLP) on your behalf, this way you are legally protected from most business liabilities. I will discuss more about each type of entities in the next chapter.

You can also go on websites like leaglzoom.com and have them draw up the document for less than what an attorney would charge you to do the same. Once you file you file the article to incorporate your business, next step is to get an accountant or CPA to file and obtain an EIN(Employer's Identification Number) from IRS. This is similar to social security number but for business. Once you have these two documents, you can then open a commercial bank account at any local bank.

Next step would be to go to your local city office and find out what type of business and regulatory licenses you are required to have. It should take a day or two to get your licenses and permits in place, and then you are finally and officially in business.

Once you have a business license and a trademark name, customers will trust your products and be more likely to buy them.

COMPETITIVE ANALYSIS

This is key to having a successful business. When you have a competitive analysis, you know your business's current position within the pet bakery industry.
The competitive analysis allows you to get the information you need on your competitors, market share, market strategies, growth and other important factors. When you have all this information, you will be able to change or improve

your business in key areas so you can increase profits and sales.

Here is a simple way you can do a competitive analysis. On a piece of paper write down the following:

1. Number of local competitors you have
2. What is their niche/what type of pet foods they sell
3. Where they sell
4. What is their pricing

Once you have that list, take a look and see where you would fit in that list, how can you stand out from the crowd, what can you do differently that would make customers pay attention to your products.

In my business experience, I believe there are three ways you can always stand above the crowd. I always have tried to stand above the crowd by trying of these three strategies.

1. By making superior products than my competitors make

2. By offering 100% customer satisfaction guarantee
3. By creative pricing strategy

Let me explain what I mean by creative pricing strategy.

CREATIVE PRICING STRATEGY

Pricing is the most important factor of your business. A carefully thought out pricing strategy can make you very successful but a pricing strategy that places you above your market can literality put you out of business and on the other hand pricing below the market can wipe your bottom line profit completely clean, and before you know it, you are out of business and in debt.

That was the risky part; now the tricky part is if you stay with the market, then you are standing out in the crowd instead you are standing in the crowd. To make yourself more visible and unique and to stand tall among other competitors, you have to be really very creative when it comes to your pricing strategy, and that is where the tricky part comes is. My goal is to teach you how to implement a carefully thought out pricing strategy that can make you stand out and make you successful.

Here are few ideas I often try:

1. Always run one special where you offer discount on one particular type of baked foods each month, but never on the same type of foods.
2. Run BOGO (Buy One Get One Free) promotion every few months on select baked items (usually the ones that are not selling fast)
3. Never try to be the low price leader (It is a slippery slope, don't try to reduce your price just to stay competitive)
4. Run various package promotion during holidays (I usually make baskets with few of our top selling goodies all nicely wrapped)

Remember, when it comes to pricing or marketing ideas, there is no "one size fits all," not every idea works for everyone. Some strategies may work better for you than others and vice versa. So, it is a good idea to test each idea separately and document the results then analyze and see which one worked the best.

UNDERSTANDING PENNY PROFIT, PROFIT MARGIN, AND MARKUP

In business these are the three most common terms we hear every day, but what do they all mean and how they are different from each other, is a question many of you have. I know this because I get email time to time about this very topic.

Okay let's break them down and see what they are:

PENNY PROFIT

Penny profit is essentially the actual cash profit you make by selling any items in your store. For example, say you just sold a bottle of 20 oz. Coke $1.75, what is the penny profit of that sale? To find the answer first, we need to see how much you paid to buy that bottle of Coke. Looking at your invoice from Coke shows you paid $1.00 for that bottle of coke and you sold it for $1.75. So your penny profit is $1.75-1.00 = 75 cents. Penny profit is the difference between the selling price- actual costs.

PROFIT MARGIN

Profit margin the term most widely used and understood in most every business as it is what we all use to figure out if we are making enough profit from our businesses by selling the products and services.

Profit margin is essentially the percentage of profit you make or earn when you sell a product. Confusing? Let's take a look at the same example of that bottle of coke we just used earlier.

We already know the penny profit from that sale was 75 cents. Now the profit margin is done little differently, to find out the exact margin we will have to take the penny profit and divide that number by the selling price. So it will be $1.75-$1.00=0.75, then we divide that penny profit by the selling price 0.75/$1.75 = 43% profit margin.

MARKUP

The markup, on the other hand, is somewhat similar to profit margin, but instead of dividing the penny profit by the selling price you would have to divide the penny profit by the actual cost. Let's take a look at the same example once again.

Remember our penny profit from that bottle ok Coke? It was 75 cents; now we just need to divide that by the actual cost which was a $1.00 right? Let's do this, 0.75/$1.00 = 75% Markup for that same bottle of Coke.

BUSINESS FORECASTING

This is another valuable business tool if you want to have a profitable business. Business forecasting is essential to determining sales targets. A month-by-month sales forecast helps you to identify problems and opportunities.

An accurate sales forecast along with a well-structured sales plan will help you to have an effective business.

CHAPTER 11: CHOOSE THE CORPORATE STRUCTURE FOR YOU

Before you submit your business plan to potential lenders, you'll need to decide what type of business structure you'll create for the benefit of the lender. Right now, your best bet is to know what your options are.

If you're working out of your home, you'll probably choose the simplest. That doesn't mean that your bakery must remain a sole proprietorship forever. As your firm grows, you may want to change the structure.

Below is a brief description of your choices. As you approach the time you need to make a decision, don't forget to get both legal and financial opinions.

SOLE PROPRIETORSHIP

As long as you're working out of your time for you. The term sole proprietorship best describes this business model. It usually indicates, as you've probably surmised, that there's only one owner who also runs the day-to-day activities of the pet bakery. You'll also be glad to hear that from a tax viewpoint, it's a good choice. You can file your taxes of the business– your income and profits– as part of your personal income.

As with any option, you run into at least a few disadvantages, and the sole proprietorship is no different. If you describe yourself as a sole proprietorship, it indicates that you personally take responsibility for any of your company's liabilities.

You may also find it difficult to raise money for your pet bakery if you choose this route. There are some lenders who are hesitant to loan money to a company that relies only on one person for its day to day operations.

Barring a loan from a bank means that if you want to raise money, you'll have to tap into your personal savings or be creative (and brave) in asking your friends and families to invest in your dream.

PARTNERSHIP

If you plan to open your pet bakery with one or more persons, then you'll want to spend some time looking at the partnership business structure. This category is divided into two categories most often called general and limited.

If you register your company as a general partnership, that means that those who have been identified as the legal partners actually are in charge of running your pet bakery and you all assume responsibility the company's debts and other obligations.

This is in contrast to a limited partnership, which has both general and limited partners. As in the general version, general partners are owners and actually operate the pet bakery. Which means that they are liable for any and all debts and obligations.

Those identified as limited partners are only investors. They don't control the functioning of the company and therefore aren't subject to the same liabilities of the general partners.

The limited partnership is not usually the first choice for a young company. The only way most individuals even consider this option is if they plan to have multiple passive investors.

Another reason why many new businesses avoid this plan is because of what's viewed as the onerous amount of paperwork that's associated with this choice.

One of the reasons so many individuals choose this route is because of the tax status it provides. A partnership doesn't have to pay taxes on its income. Instead, the tax liability merely "passes through" any profits or losses the individual partners make. When tax time rolls around, the partnership files a tax return. Then, the partners themselves report their share of any profit or loss on their personal returns.

Of course, there are a few disadvantages to this structure. The first difficulty is that all general partners are personally responsible for any liability created and held by the business itself in this form.

The general partner can act on behalf of the pet bakery, take out loans, and make decisions on behalf of the business that are binding on behalf of all the partners. But more than that, you'll find that the partnership costs more when it comes to the initial setup for it.

CORPORATION

It just might be you have a friend or relative who believes themselves to be knowledgeable in this area, and they might try to talk you into structuring your business under the auspices of a corporation.

If you aren't a seasoned businessperson, then you probably want to hold filing under this determination. In the eyes of the law, a corporation is viewed as a legal entity separate from any of its owners. You should know right off the start that it's one of the most expensive options. Not to mention, the corporation is mandated by more rules and regulations than some of the other business structures.

So, with these disadvantages, what would attract it to any entrepreneur? The biggest benefit is the liability protection that comes with structure. When you model your business this way, you don't have to worry about your personal responsibility for any liability. You don't have to be concerned that if the corporation gets sued, your personal savings and other investments will not be at risk. In other words, the court can't force you to turn your personal savings and collateral in order to pay the bills.

One of the more advantageous reasons for forming as a corporation is the ability to raise money relatively easily. If your business is a corporation, then the company can sell stock to raise funds. Some individuals like the corporation as a business structure because it continues on indefinitely, regardless of the circumstances of any of the shareholders.

If a shareholder dies, for example, the shares they held are sold, or they become what's called disabled

However, many individuals who are just starting up avoid this structure, partly because of the cost of getting your business legally set up in this structure. But wait, you may think that higher costs that go a long way to safeguarding your personal funds would be worth the extra money. When you're struggling through with some of the more mundane aspects of starting the business, it's easy to see how you could put this in the back of your mind, with the option of organizing in this fashion later.

Whether you decide– either today or down the road– to create a corporation, there is one disadvantage you'll also run head to head with. Be prepared to pay a double tax. A corporation is the only structure that is subject to taxes on both federal and state levels. The corporation pays the taxes, and when the company distributes the profits in the form of dividends, the individual shareholders must report and pay taxes on it.

THE S CORPORATION

There is a version of the corporation that appeals to many smaller business owners. You may find that, depending on the growth of your venture, you may want to take a serious look at this method of organizing your financial assets.

This version has a few more advantageous tax rules while simultaneously providing you with the liability protection. In this structure, profit and losses of the corporation aren't taxed at the corporate level. Instead, they are only passed through to the shareholders and then revealed on their personal tax forms.

While this sounds good, before you sign on the dotted line you should be aware of the downside of the business structure. They may be a different type of corporation, but they are still, nonetheless subject to many of the same tax laws.

Additionally, this type of corporation can only issue one type of stock, and its shareholders are limited to 100.

LIMITED LIABILITY COMPANY

This structure just recently celebrated its 40th birthday, having been created in 1977, making it the youngest of the business structures. This entity was created to try to put the best parts of the partnership corporate models into one structure. Unlike the corporation, this is not subjected to double taxation. Earnings and losses are simply passed through to the owners and then are placed only on their personal taxes. At the same time, the partners enjoy limited liability as in the original corporate structure.

You may not have to choose right at this moment what structure you prefer for your shop, but by the time you file the business plan, you'll have to declare the structure. It's best to talk to a trusted accountant or even an attorney. Either of these can walk you through the benefits and disadvantages of each of these structures. He or she will also be able to offer you some advice after you talk about your personal circumstances.

EIN FROM IRS

EIN or Employer Identification number is essentially a social security or tax identification number but for your business. IRS and many other governmental agencies can identify your business via this unique 9 digit number.

Remember you will not need this number if you choose to be a sole proprietorship for your business.

It is simple to apply, either you can do it yourself or get your accountant to apply for you, but the process is simple, you fill out the form SS-4, which can be filed online, via Fax or via mail.

Here is a link to IRS website where you can download or fill out the form online. https://www.irs.gov/businesses/small-businesses-self-employed/how-to-apply-for-an-ein

OPENING A COMMERCIAL BANK ACCOUNT

This is one important step, but it can only be done after you have a fully executed article of incorporation which has been approved by the state, and you have an EIN number assigned by the IRS.

Once you have these two documents, you should be able to go to a bank and open your first commercial bank account.

But remember to check and understand various types of commercial checking account fees, you want to find a bank that offers free or almost free commercial checking account because some larger banks can charge you hundreds of dollars each month depending on how many transactions you do. Make sure to ask and shop around before you sign on the dotted line.

CHAPTER 12: REMINDERS ON STATE AND LOCAL REGULATIONS

I've left this chapter for one of the last ones to talk about. That doesn't mean it's unimportant. In fact, while it may be a less-than-inspiring chapter and certainly doesn't appeal to the creative side of your entrepreneurial spirit, it's crucial to be aware of this information before you launch your pet bakery business.

You're certainly planning on making meals for pets, but your bakery's products fall within the range of the pet-food business. This means that your firm must meet all regulations that business requires.

While there are several federal rules, most of these regulations are mandated by state and well . . . right there you realize no two states are going to do anything alike. But before you moan and start heading for Google, we can at least organize the categories, even just a bit.

TAKE BUSINESS REGISTRATION

This is one regulation that probably can be found regardless of the state in which you live. Pet-food manufacturers must register their labels with the U.S. Department of Agriculture.

But wait, you can't register your label until you get a feed license. Requirements for this license do differ from state to state. If you live and plan to open your business in Texas, for example, you'll need to register your pet food and license your facility itself.

In California, though, licenses are mandated for each retail location you own, as well as the manufacturing facility. Then there's Iowa, in which the company that owns the dog food label needs to be licensed, as well as each product.

If this doesn't get your head spinning, this option certainly will help. In a few states, you can register for a two-year license.

REGULATIONS FOR THE PET FOOD

Here again, you have a conglomerate of various regulations that differ from state to state. This, is in addition to any rules and regulations the federal government mandates as well.

Pet food, which is what your bakery falls under, is considered part of the animal feed category. Such items mandated under this umbrella include commercial food, treats, nutrient supplements, and edible chews.

In this area of regulations, you'll find that the AAFCO has a set of federal guidelines in its publications.

These guidelines are also the basis of the states' animal-feed laws. Surprisingly, there are two states that don't have established pet food laws: Nevada and Alaska.

But nothing is ever complete in the food business– even the pet food business– until the US FDA has weighed in with its mandates as well. The FDA maintains that foods which use unapproved colorings intended for the animal, as well as humans, are considered "adulterated" as long as they are made with color additives. The FDA has clearly defined regulations about what these are.

SALES LAWS

Your pet bakery business will also have to follow a set of sales laws. And again, you guessed it; these differ from state to state.

Most states require you apply and receive a business license before you begin selling the treats. If you're selling your products online, you're limited to selling to customers in which you are already registered.

Unfortunately, there is not a central agency that can grant you approval to sell in all of the states. If you're selling your treats at local farmers' market, you also have to follow a specific set of regulations which vary throughout the nation.

LABELS: FDA RULES

The FDA says that pet food sold in the United States must be pure and wholesome, contain no harmful or deleterious substances, and be truthfully labeled.

This means you must clearly identify the product first as pet food, as well as providing a quantity statement. This is a list of all of the ingredients in your treat in the order of quantity or weight. The first ingredient listed needs to be the one that either weighs the most or is the largest according to your recipe. Let's say your treat contains three ingredients, like peanut butter, oatmeal, and honey. If there is more peanut butter than either oatmeal or honey, you need to list it first.

The label should also have clear contact information for your business.

CONCLUSION: A FEW CLOSING REMARKS

Still chewing over the pros and cons of starting up a pet bakery?

That's understandable. When I was first considering it, what really convinced me were these statistics. One of my reasons for my hesitations in starting the business was my fear that doggie and pet bakeries were merely a passing fad. I feared it was a flash in the pan and I would jump in only to find others bailing because customers, now former customers, have flocked to another trend, deeming it more attractive.

My fears were calmed when I read this– which by the way is hanging in my home bakery pantry. I make it a habit of reading it every day, comforted in the fact that this industry has no place to go but up.

The United States pet industry made $50.84 billion in the year 2011, according to statistics gathered by the Pet Product Manufacturers Association. Of that number, pet food captured nearly 20 million dollars more than that– nearly half of all the money spent on pets in general.

The same organization also estimated that there were currently 78 million dogs and 86 million cats in the United States.

If those aren't encouraging news, nothing is. Of course, the forecast for the future is for even more spending.

Fear of being burned by a sudden drain of customers shouldn't be a concern at all. In fact, I'm betting after reading that, you're already scribbling your notes for your launch.

GROW YOUR BUSINESS TO YOUR OWN SIZE

Whether you're planning on starting small from your home, using local and regional marketing plans with an initial online presence, or creating your own retail outlet, keep in mind there really is no right or wrong way to begin. As long as you realize that success depends on your intention to succeed.

I've learned that a long time ago, and before I even talk about my pet bakery success to those individuals who ask me about my story, I give them the few steps I use before I ordered one piece of equipment or even created a business card– I run through my intentions and commitment to the project.

Though people promise to help and to take the risk, there will inevitably be a time where you will find few people could help at the exact moment you needed them.

How will you react? Will you throw your hands in the air and give up, or will you find a way to overcome that hurdle and viewing it only as a small bump in the road. Your reaction will give you valuable insight about whether you're committed to your business.

Once you decide that your intention is to succeed, then your next step is to visualize your view of success. The definition of success is typically the same for each of us– even those who share the desire to launch a pet bakery.

It could be that you're dreaming big and then visualizing big. A large retail store? Go for it.

But if your real dreams hold a more modest definition of success, that's all right too. It could be that all you really want– at least at the moment– is a business that allows you a few more extra dollars every week to help pay the bills or buy groceries. Or maybe you're looking for a way to take control of your own life and spend more time with your family.

Your idea of success could also be a modest online presence and a healthy local business.

After that, you can put the ideas in this book into action, and never give up.

Good luck!

Made in the USA
Coppell, TX
01 February 2024

28489133R00098